A Kid's Guide to Drawing America™

How to Draw
North Dakota's
Sights and Symbols

Melody S. Mis

The Rosen Publishing Group's
PowerKids Press™
New York

To my father, Joseph J. Mis, who made it possible for me to pursue a career in writing

Published in 2002 by The Rosen Publishing Group, Inc.
29 East 21st Street, New York, NY 10010

First Edition

Editor: Jannell Khu
Book Design: Kim Sonsky
Layout Design: Nick Sciacca

Illustration Credits: Laura Murawski
Photo Credits: p. 7 courtesy of the International Peace Garden; pp. 8–9 courtesy of Oscar & Luella Buros Center for Testing, University of Nebraska—Lincoln, Lincoln, NE; pp. 12, 14 © One Mile Up, Incorporated; p. 16 © Michael Maconachie; Papilio/CORBIS; p. 18 © W. Perry Conway/CORBIS; p. 20 © Eric and David Hosking/CORBIS; pp. 22, 28 © Index Stock; p. 24 © Paul A. Souders/CORBIS; p. 26 © David Muench/CORBIS.

Mis, Melody S.
How to draw North Dakota's sights and symbols / Melody S. Mis.
p. cm. — (A kid's guide to drawing America)
Includes index.
Summary: This book explains how to draw some of North Dakota's sights and symbols, including the state seal and the official flower.
  ISBN 0-8239-6090-0
1. Emblems, State—North Dakota—Juvenile literature 2. North Dakota—In art—Juvenile literature   3. Drawing—Technique—Juvenile literature   [1. Emblems, State—North Dakota   2. North Dakota   3. Drawing—Technique]
I. Title   II. Series
  2002
  743'.8'99784—dc21

Manufactured in the United States of America

CONTENTS

Let's Draw North Dakota

In the 1600s, when the French explored the area that would become North Dakota, it was inhabited by the Great Northern Plains Indians. These Native Americans were expert animal trappers. They used animal pelts for clothes and traded them to the French for guns and food. By the early 1800s, fur trade had become the first major business in the North Dakota area. Beaver pelts were especially in demand and were sent to Europe and to America's East Coast states.

Mandan and Hidatsa Native Americans lived in the Knife River Indian villages. The villages were the main markets for fur trade in the early 1800s. Today you can visit the Knife River Indian Villages National Historic Site in Stanton, North Dakota.

Knife River was one of the places where explorers Lewis and Clark stopped on their expedition, which lasted from 1804 to 1806. They explored land that the United States had purchased from France in 1803, called the Louisiana Purchase. The expedition traveled from Missouri to the Pacific Coast and back. This was the first expedition that the United States undertook. At

Knife River, Lewis and Clark hired French fur trader Toussaint Charbonneau and his young Native American wife, Sacagawea, to guide them in their expedition. Sacagawea knew many Native American languages. She acted as an interpreter and helped Lewis and Clark to forge friendships with other Native Americans.

This book will show you how to draw some of North Dakota's sights and symbols. Directions are under each step, and new steps are shown in red. Before you start to draw, you will need the following supplies:

- A sketch pad
- An eraser
- A number 2 pencil
- A pencil sharpener

These are some of the shapes and drawing terms you need to know to draw North Dakota's sights and symbols:

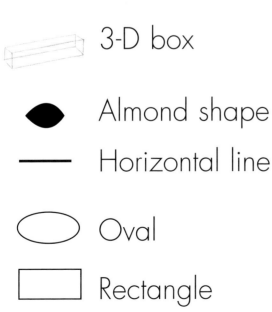

3-D box

 Shading

Almond shape

Squiggle

Horizontal line

Teardrop

Oval

Vertical line

Rectangle

 Wavy line

The Peace Garden State

The longest unfortified border in the world lies between the United States and Canada. In 1932, North Dakota and Manitoba, Canada, created a garden to link both countries called the International Peace Garden. This garden celebrates the friendship between the United States and Canada.

At the International Peace Garden, you will see the Peace Tower, the Peace Chapel, and even a huge working clock called the floral clock. With the exception of the clock hands, the clock is decorated and made entirely with flowers!

In 1956, North Dakota's Motor Vehicle Department put "Peace Garden State" on automobile license plates. The name was so popular that the North Dakota legislature adopted it as the state's nickname in 1957. North Dakota is also called the Flickertail State because there are so many ground squirrels, or flickertails, in the state. These squirrels are called flickertails because they flick, or jerk, their tails when they run into their burrows.

The International Peace Garden is located between North Dakota and Canada. Each year, more than one quarter of a million people from around the world visit the garden.

Artist in North Dakota

Luella Gubrud Buros

Luella Gubrud Buros was born in Canby, Minnesota, in 1901. When she was two years old, her parents moved to North Dakota. In 1931, Buros began her art studies at New York's Columbia University. Buros received many awards for her paintings. Many of her paintings were displayed in museums, such as the Metropolitan Museum of Art in New York City.

Some of Buros's favorite landscapes to sketch and paint were of the North Dakota prairies where she spent her childhood. Painted around 1940, *North Dakota Farm* shows her realistic painting style. This means Buros painted the cold, bare farm scene exactly as she saw it. What makes

Buros sketched *North Dakota Farm* circa 1940. It is a graphite-on-paper sketch. Artists often sketch before painting their subject matters.

the painting interesting is that Buros also saw the quiet, peaceful beauty in the landscape, which she sensitively captured, in a realistic way.

The artist and her husband, Oscar, traveled throughout Africa in 1956–1957. Buros took photographs in Africa, many of African women. Before her death in 1995, Buros left most of her paintings and more than 14,000 photographs of Africa to the University of Nebraska. Today the largest collection of Buros's paintings hangs in the Buros Institute at the University of Nebraska.

North Dakota Farm is an oil-on-canvas work that measures 25" x 31" (63.5 cm x 79 cm). Buros spent her childhood on a farm like the one above. She once said, "I'm a country girl. My childhood home was a farm in North Dakota. My father had a huge wheat field there."

Map of North Dakota

Map of the Continental United States

There are three regions in North Dakota. The Red River Valley region is on the eastern side of the state, where the state's major crops grow. In the middle of the state is the Drift Prairie region. This region has rolling prairies and lakes. The town of Rugby is in this region. Many consider Rugby to be the center of the North American continent! Between the Missouri River and the western border of North Dakota is the Missouri Plateau region. This is the area of the Great Plains. White Butte is the state's highest point at 3,506 feet (1,069 m) above sea level. The Theodore Roosevelt National Park and the Badlands are in the Missouri Plateau region. The Badlands are famous for their colorful canyons, rock formations, and buttes.

1

Begin with a rectangle. The right side of the rectangle has a slight angle.

2

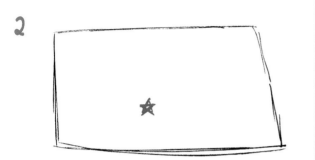

Draw a five-pointed star for the capital, Bismarck.

3

On the right side of the rectangle, draw a circle for the city of Fargo.

4

Draw six pointed shapes for White Butte.

5

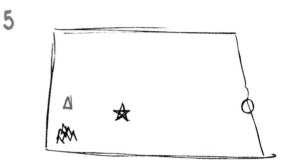

Add a triangle for Theodore Roosevelt National Park.

⭐	Bismarck
△	Theodore Roosevelt National Park
▭	Fort Union Trading Post
⋀⋀⋀	White Butte
○	Fargo

6

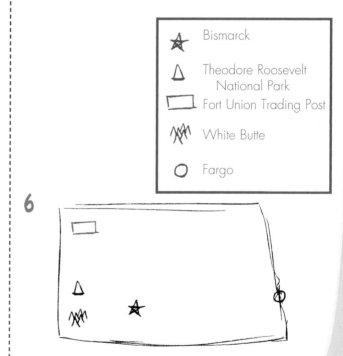

Draw a rectangle for the Fort Union Trading Post. You can also draw the map key if you'd like.

11

The State Seal

In the center of North Dakota's seal are a tree, three bundles of wheat, and a plow. These images stand for the state's agriculture. To the bottom left of the tree is a bow with three arrows. Above the arrows, a Native American on horseback chases a buffalo. Native Americans used every part of the buffalo for food, clothing, and shelter. This scene honors the Native Americans. At the time the seal was designed, North Dakota had not yet become the thirty-ninth state to join the Union. It is assumed that the 42 stars represent the number of states that would be admitted to the Union by the end of 1889. Above the stars is North Dakota's motto. Written around the circle is October 1, 1889. This is the date North Dakota adopted its constitution.

1

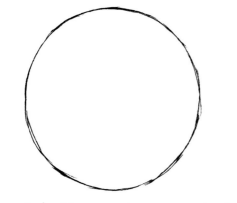

Draw a circle. You can draw around a lid of a jar as a guide.

2

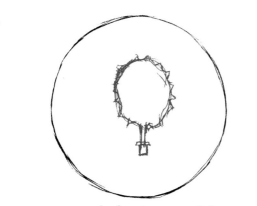

Draw a wavy circle for the top of the tree and a narrow rectangle for the trunk. Then draw two more rectangles at the base of the tree.

3

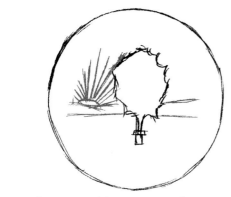

Draw a horizontal line across the center of the large circle. Draw a slanted line on each side of the tree. Next draw the sun. For the sun rays, draw lines that fan out from the sun.

4

Study the buffalo and the man on horseback. First draw the buffalo. Next use circles and rectangles to draw the man and the horse. Draw a vertical line on the right.

5

Draw a vertical line near the buffalo. Add detail to the man and the horse. In the lower left, draw the bow and three arrows. Next draw the chopping block. Make the plow on the right side of the circle.

6

Add the two rows of five-pointed stars, then shade in the tree and the sun's rays. Add shadows under the buffalo, the horse, the tree, the chopping block, and the plow.

The State Flag

North Dakota's state flag was adopted on March 3, 1911. A bald eagle, the nation's symbol of freedom, is in the center of the flag. Bald eagles are found only in America. On the eagle's chest is a red, white, and blue emblem. These are the colors of America's flag. The 13 stars above the eagle represent the 13 original colonies. The eagle has a ribbon in its beak. The words *"E Pluribus Unum"* are written on the ribbon. These words mean "one out of many." In its right claw, the eagle holds an olive branch, which stands for peace. In its left claw, the eagle holds arrows, which represent the government's military strength. Beneath the eagle, "North Dakota" is written on a scroll.

1

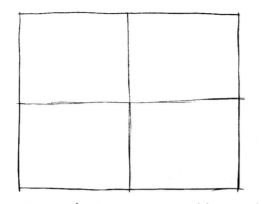

Draw a rectangle. Use one vertical line and one horizontal line to divide the rectangle into four equal sections.

2

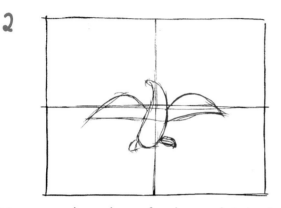

Use a teardrop shape for the eagle's body. For the wings, draw two half circles and a line underneath them. To add the eagle's legs, draw two ovals.

3

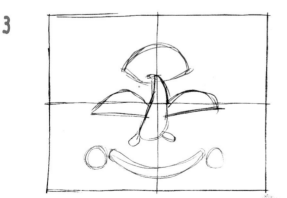

Use two curved lines to draw the sun over the eagle's head. Add two connected, curved lines underneath the eagle. Next add a circle on either side of these lines.

4

Erase extra lines. Add detail to the bird. Draw the emblem on the eagle's body. Draw the arrow in the right claw. Under the bird, draw outer circles around the first circles.

5

Shape the eagle's beak. Draw seven little triangles along the edge of the sun. Add two rows of five-pointed stars inside the sun. Draw a ribbon under the sun. Under the bird, shape the two circles into swirls.

6

Add shading and detail. Erase the extra lines. Well done!

15

The Wild Prairie Rose

In summer, the blossoms of the wild prairie rose (*Rosa blanda*) add color to North Dakota's rolling grasslands, pastures, and prairies. The flower has five bright pink petals and a yellow center. The wild prairie rose is a

small shrub. Shrubs are woody plants that are smaller than trees. The wild prairie rose can be found from the East Coast to the Great Plains of North Dakota. It grows best in cool, damp soil. Several Native American people used the fruit of the rose, called the rose hip, in medicines and in food. Rose hips are an excellent source of vitamin C. North Dakota's schoolchildren voted for the wild prairie rose to be the state flower in 1898. It was formally adopted as North Dakota's state flower in 1907.

1

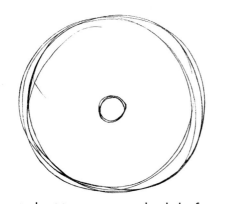

Draw a circle. You can use the lid of a jar as a guide. In the middle of that circle, draw a smaller circle.

2

Next draw the petals. They're shaped like hearts. The point of each heart touches the small circle at the center. The top of each heart touches the outside of the larger circle.

3

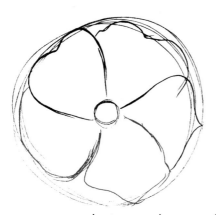

Draw two more petals. Notice how each petal has a slightly different shape.

4

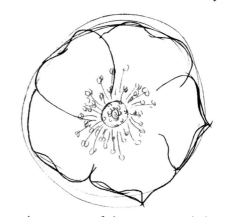

Start in the center of the rose, and draw many short lines. Add a small circle at the top of each line.

5

Shade the center of the rose. Use the tip of your pencil and make short strokes. Start at the center of the rose, and move outward.

6

Continue to shade around the center of the rose. Shade the outer edges of the petals, too. Erase any extra lines. Excellent job!

The American Elm

The American elm (*Ulmus americana*) became North Dakota's state tree in 1947. It is a large tree and can grow from 80 to 100 feet (24–30 m) tall. Several limbs branch out toward the bottom of the tree trunk. The branches spread out like a low roof and provide plenty of shade in the summer. Animals eat the elm's leaves and bark. Birds eat the elm tree's fruit. Lumber from the American elm is used to make furniture, wall paneling, and barrels. In the 1930s, a fungus spread among the nation's elm trees and killed many trees. This fungus was called Dutch elm disease. Insects spread the deadly fungus to trees from the East Coast to the Great Plains. Today American elms are once again common across the state of North Dakota.

1

Use curved lines to draw the trunk of the tree and the branches. Notice the placement of the branches.

2

Gently shade in the area around the branches and the trunk. Turn your pencil on its side, and lightly shade with short up-and-down strokes.

3

Continue to shade in the area around the branches. Notice that some areas are darker than others.

4

Now use the tip of your pencil to fill in the trunk and the larger branches. Your tree is done. Good job!

The Western Meadowlark

The western meadowlark (*Sturnella neglecta*) was chosen as North Dakota's state bird in 1947. It is a member of the blackbird family. The meadowlark has a yellow chest and a brown, spotted body. It is about 9 inches (23 cm) long. The western meadowlark is a songbird. Its loud song sounds like "wee hir weedle-ee wih-chee." When the meadowlark wants to send a short message to other birds, it makes a noise that sounds like "chuk." This sound can be used to warn other birds of danger.

The dry grasslands of North Dakota are perfect habitats for the western meadowlark. There are plenty of insects and seeds in the grasslands for the bird to eat. North Dakota farmers depend on the meadowlark to eat pesky insects that can harm crops!

1

Draw two ovals, one large and one small. These are the bird's body and head. Notice that the two ovals overlap.

2

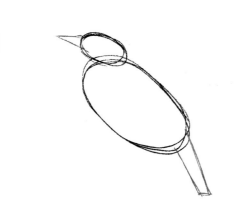

For the bird's beak, draw two lines that come to a point. For the tail, draw two parallel lines and a short line that connects them.

3

Use a narrow almond shape to draw the bird's wing. Draw straight lines for the bird's legs and feet.

4

Draw two curved lines to join the head to the body. Use an oval for the bird's eye. Draw three lines to add detail to the beak. Add details to the claws. Erase extra lines.

5

Use the drawing above as a guide. Draw straight and curved lines to form the pattern on the meadowlark's body.

6

Erase extra lines. Shade the pattern of the meadowlark. Notice that some areas are darker than others. Excellent work!

The Nokota Horse

North Dakota adopted the Nokota as its honorary horse in 1993. In the early 1600s, Native Americans captured many of these horses when they raided the Spanish explorers' camps. Native Americans and pioneers used Nokota horses for transportation and to carry goods. Today there are few Nokota horses left in North Dakota. Many died during the drought of the 1930s. In the 1960s, the last surviving herd of wild horses was found in Theodore Roosevelt National Park, North Dakota. Two brothers, Leo and Frank Kuntz, bought the Nokota horses and moved them to their ranch in North Dakota. Today you can find surviving Nokota horses at the Kuntz brothers' ranch.

1

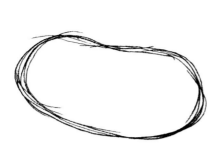

Draw a horizontal oval. This is the body of the horse.

2

To the right of the large oval, draw a smaller, vertical oval for the head. Connect the head to the body with a curved line. Add a curved triangle for the horse's tail.

3

Use narrow rectangles to draw the horse's legs. At the bottom of these narrow rectangles, draw smaller rectangles for the hooves. Notice that the hooves slant.

4

Draw in the details of the horse's face and mane. Draw lines across the hooves to separate them from the legs.

5

Fill out the tail with straight lines. Finish the hooves. Use shading and detail to finish your drawing. Notice that the mane and the tail are darker than the rest of the horse. Erase extra lines. You're done. Congratulations!

The Northern Pike

The northern pike (*Esox lucius*) became North Dakota's state fish in 1969. This is one of the most popular game fish in North Dakota. The pike is a powerful fish. It can weigh as much as 50 pounds (23 kg) and can grow to be more than 4 feet (1.2 m) long. It is greenish brown and has yellow spots on its body. It is the same color as seaweed, so other fish can't see it. This camouflage helps the pike to catch other fish to eat. The northern pike also feeds on frogs! The northern pike is a freshwater fish that is found in lakes, streams, and rivers throughout most of North America.

1

Carefully study the basic shape of the fish before you begin. Draw a straight line on top and a curved line on the bottom. The right side will be the tail.

2

For the head, draw a curved vertical line. Next draw the open mouth. Draw a curved line for the tail.

3

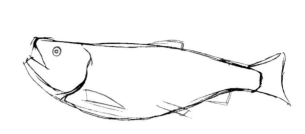

For the eye, draw a circle and then draw a smaller circle inside the first circle. Draw five fins on the sides of the fish.

4

Erase any extra lines. Now begin shading. Hold your pencil at an angle and lightly shade the fish with up-and-down strokes. Notice that some parts of the fish are darker than others.

The Covered Wagon

In the 1840s, pioneers migrated to North Dakota and the American West. They traveled in covered wagons for as long as six months. The wagons were strong and were large enough to carry a family and all of their possessions. Hooks throughout the wagon held guns, bonnets, milk cans, and other items. Large, wooden hoops were curved, or bent, over the wagon. A canvas cloth was stretched over these hoops, and oil was rubbed into the cloth to make it waterproof. Two buckets were kept under the wagon. One held grease to keep the wheels turning easily. The other held coals to light campfires. The pioneers brought enough food to last for the entire journey.

1

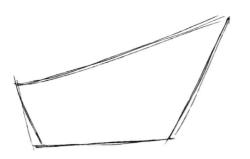

Draw the shape above. Notice that the top of the shape is wider than the bottom. This is the basic shape of the wagon.

2

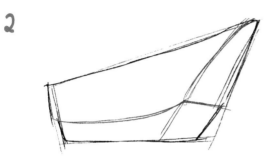

Draw straight and curved lines within the shape to define the bottom, the top, and the side of the wagon.

3

Draw three circles for the wheels. The fourth wheel is hidden, so you don't need to draw it!

4

Draw eight curved lines that go from the top to the bottom of the wagon. Notice that these lines look like candy canes. Add a triangle and a narrow oval to the front of the wagon.

5

Now add two 3-D boxes to the wagon. Draw a wide one on the front and a narrow one on the side. Add the other details shown in red.

6

Erase the middle of the lines that look like candy canes. Add straight lines to make the wheel spokes. Shade and add detail to finish.

North Dakota's Capitol

The state capitol of North Dakota is a tall, modern building. At 19 stories high, it is called the skyscraper of the plains. The current capitol was built in 1932, after the first capitol burned down. The new capitol was built during the Great Depression, a period of unemployment and poverty in America. It had to be a simple building that wouldn't cost too much to build. Architects from North Dakota and Chicago designed the capitol in the art deco style. This style is not ornate and has simple lines and shapes. Many different kinds of materials were used inside the building. The lobby floor is made of marble. Many of the rooms are paneled in exotic woods, including mahogany from Honduras and oak from England.

1

Draw a narrow, horizontal rectangle.

2

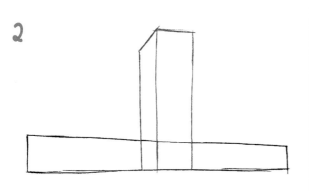

Add two tall, vertical rectangles to the middle of the horizontal rectangle. Notice how one side of the left vertical rectangle is shorter than the other side.

3

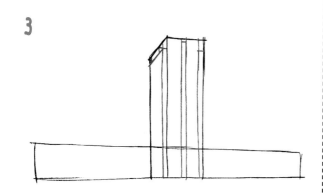

Add four vertical lines to the tall rectangles. Use horizontal lines to add the other details.

4

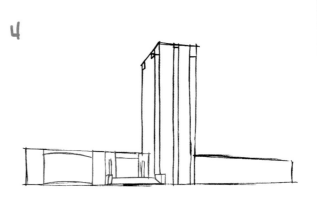

Use straight and curved lines to add more details to the capitol building.

5

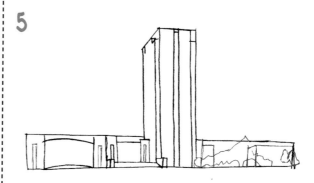

Continue to add details to the horizontal rectangle. Add trees to the right side of the capitol. Notice that the big tree has a basic triangle shape. Erase any extra lines.

6

Shade the building. Hold your pencil at an angle, and use soft strokes. Super job!

North Dakota State Facts

Statehood	November 2, 1889, 39th state
Area	70,704 square miles (183,122.5 sq km)
Population	633,700
Capital	Bismarck, population, 53,500
Most Populated City	Fargo, population, 77,100
Industries	Oil, coal, natural gas
Agriculture	Wheat, barley, sunflowers, pinto beans, cattle, hogs, honeybees
Nicknames	The Peace Garden State, the Flickertail State, the Sioux State
Motto	Liberty And Union, Now And Forever, One And Inseparable
Flower	Wild prairie rose
Tree	American elm
Grass	Western wheatgrass
Bird	Western meadowlark
Honorary horse	Nokota horse
Fish	Northern pike
Fossil	Teredo petrified wood
Beverage	Milk
Song	"North Dakota Hymn"
Dance	Square dance

30

Glossary

ancient (AYN-chent) Very old. From a very long time ago.

buttes (BYOOTS) A mountain or hill that stands alone.

camouflage (KAH-muh-flahj) A disguise to make something look like its surroundings.

canyons (KAN-yuhns) Deep valleys that have steep sides.

continent (KON-tin-ent) One of Earth's seven large land masses.

descendants (dih-SEN-dents) People or animals born of a certain family or group.

drought (DROWT) A long period of dry weather that generally hurts crops.

emblem (EM-bluhm) A picture with a motto.

extinction (ik-STINK-shun) When something no longer exists.

exotic (ik-ZAH-tik)   Foreign, strange, and unusual.

expedition (ek-spuh-DIH-shun) A journey made for a particular reason.

fungus (FUN-guhs) Simple plants that do not have leaves or roots.

Great Depression (GRAYT de-PREH-shun) A time in the 1930s when banks and businesses lost money, causing many people to lose their jobs.

habitats (HA-bih-tats) Surroundings where an animal or a plant naturally lives.

legislature (LEH-jihs-lay-chur) A body of persons that has the power to make or pass laws.

paneling (PA-nuhl-ing) Flat, thin pieces of wood or other material used to cover walls.

pelts (PELTZ) Animal skins with the fur still on them.

plateau (pla-TOH) A flat area of land.

prairies (PRAIR-eez) Grasslands.

skyscraper (SKY-skray-pur) A very tall building.

symbol (SIM-bul) An object or a design that stands for something important.

unfortified (un-FOR-tuh-fyd) Not defended against possible attack.

Index

Web Sites

To learn more about North Dakota, check out these Web sites:
www.ndtourism.com/attractions.html
www.ndtourism.com/regions/west/WestDino.html